Presented to _Karen Glenna_
" Happy 20th Birthday
September 21, 1990

From _Love forever_   Mum & Dad
                              x x x o o

BY Helen Steiner Rice

HELEN STEINER RICE

Always a Springtime

Poems of Hope and Renewal

Fleming H. Revell Company
Old Tappan, New Jersey

The poems in this volume were previously published in the books *Prayerfully* and *Life Is Forever.*

Jacket and interior illustrations by Steffi Karen Rubin.

Library of Congress Cataloging-in-Publication Data
Rice, Helen Steiner.
   Always a springtime.

   "Previously published in the books Prayerfully and Life is forever"—T.P. verso.
   1. Christian poetry, American. I. Rice, Helen Steiner. Life is forever. 1987. II. Title.
PS3568.I28P7   1987   811'.54   87-12675
ISBN 0-8007-1556-X

Illustrations Copyright © 1987 by Steffi Karen Rubin
Text Copyright © 1987 by The Helen Steiner Rice Foundation
Published by the Fleming H. Revell Company
Old Tappan, New Jersey, 07675
Printed in the United States of America

Always a Springtime

Poems of Hope and Renewal

CONTENTS

Poems of Renewal

Introduction

Every spring, the earth is renewed. The bleak winter is left behind, and all nature begins to reawaken and blossom. This is the season of hope.

As tulips are signs of spring, prayer is evidence of hope. Prayer is communicating with the One who is our hope. In times of gladness or times of turmoil, during seasons of peace or days of crisis, our hearts turn to God to rejoice in our happiness or to seek guidance for our troubles.

Each morning can bring new hope as we draw closer to God. Prayer teaches us to rely daily on His goodness. We learn to enjoy His presence and to seek Him out.

Helen Steiner Rice began each day with this prayer:

> *Bless me, Heavenly Father,*
> *Forgive my erring ways,*
> *Grant me strength to serve Thee,*
> *Put purpose in my days . . .*
> *Give me understanding*
> *Enough to make me kind*
> *So I may judge all people*
> *With my heart and not my mind . . .*
> *And teach me to be patient*
> *In everything I do,*
> *Content to trust your wisdom*
> *And to follow after You . . .*
> *And help me when I falter*
> *And hear me when I pray*
> *And receive me in Thy Kingdom*
> *To dwell with Thee some day.*

May her prayer become yours, and may each of these poems draw you closer to His Love.

Good Morning, God!

You are ushering in another day
Untouched and freshly new
So here I come to ask You, God,
If You'll renew me, too,
Forgive the many errors
That I made yesterday
And let me try again, dear God,
To walk closer in Thy way . . .
But, Father, I am well aware
I can't make it on my own
So take my hand and hold it tight
For I can't walk alone!

It's Me Again, God

Remember me, God?
I come every day
Just to talk with You, Lord,
And to learn how to pray . . .
You make me feel welcome,
You reach out Your hand,
I need never explain
For You understand . . .
I come to You frightened
And burdened with care
So lonely and lost
And so filled with despair,
And suddenly, Lord,
I'm no longer afraid,
My burden is lighter
And the dark shadows fade . . .
Oh, God, what a comfort
To know that You care
And to know when I seek You
You will always be there!

Daily Prayers Are "Heaven's Stairs"

The "Stairway" rises "Heaven high"—
The "steps" are dark and steep,
In weariness we climb them
As we stumble, fall, and weep . . .
And many times we falter
Along the "path of prayer"
Wondering if You hear us
And if You really care . . .
Oh, give us some assurance,
Restore our faith anew,
So we can keep on climbing
The "Stairs of Prayer" to You—
For we are weak and wavering,
Uncertain and unsure,
And only meeting You in prayer
Can help us to endure
All life's trials and troubles
Its sickness, pain, and sorrow,
And give us strength and courage
To face and meet tomorrow!

What Is Prayer?

Is it measured words that are memorized,
Forcefully said and dramatized,
Offered with pomp and with arrogant pride
In words unmatched to the feelings inside?
No . . . prayer is so often just words unspoken
Whispered in tears by a heart that is broken . . .
For God is already deeply aware
Of the burdens we find too heavy to bear,
And all we need do is to seek Him in prayer
And without a word He will help us to bear
Our trials and troubles—our sickness and sorrow
And show us the way to a brighter tomorrow . . .
There's no need at all for impressive prayer
For the minute we seek God He is already there!

God, Are You There?

I'm way down here!
You're way up there!
Are You sure You can hear
My faint, faltering prayer?
For I'm so unsure
Of just how to pray—
To tell you the truth, God,
I don't know what to say . . .
I just know I am lonely
And vaguely disturbed,
Bewildered and restless,
Confused and perturbed . . .
And they tell me that prayer
Helps to quiet the mind
And to unburden the heart
For in stillness we find
A newborn assurance
That Someone does care
And Someone does answer
Each small sincere prayer!

The Mystery of Prayer

Beyond that which words can interpret
Or theology can explain
The soul feels a "shower of refreshment"
That falls like the gentle rain
On hearts that are parched with problems
And are searching to find the way
To somehow attract God's attention
Through well-chosen words as they pray,
Not knowing that God in His wisdom
Can sense all man's worry and woe
For there is nothing man can conceal
That God does not already know . . .
So kneel in prayer in His presence
And you'll find no need to speak
For softly in silent communion
God grants you the peace that you seek.

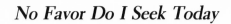

No Favor Do I Seek Today

I come not to ask, to plead, or implore You,
I just come to tell You how much I adore You,
For to kneel in Your Presence makes me feel blest
For I know that You know all my needs best . . .
And it fills me with joy just to linger with You
As my soul You replenish and my heart You renew,
For prayer is much more than just asking for things—
It's the Peace and Contentment that Quietness brings . . .
So thank You again for Your mercy and love
And for making me heir to Your Kingdom above!

Finding Faith in a Flower

Sometimes when faith is running low
And I cannot fathom why things are so . . .
I walk alone among the flowers I grow
And learn the "answers" to all I would know!
For among my flowers I have come to see
Life's miracle and its mystery . . .
And standing in silence and reverie
My faith comes flooding back to me!

My Garden of Prayer

My garden beautifies my yard
    and adds fragrance to the air . . .
But it is also my cathedral
    and my quiet place of prayer . . .
So little do we realize
    that "The Glory and The Power"
Of He who made the universe
    lies hidden in a flower.

"What Has Been Is What Will Be . . . and There Is Nothing New Under the Sun"

(ECCLESIASTES 1:9)

Today my soul is reaching out
For something that's unknown,
I cannot grasp or fathom it
For it's known to God alone—
I cannot hold or harness it
Or put it into form,
For it's as uncontrollable
As the wind before the storm—
I know not where it came from
Or whither it will go,
For it's as inexplicable
As the restless winds that blow—
And like the wind it too will pass
And leave nothing more behind
Than the "memory of a mystery"
That blew across my mind—
But like the wind it will return
To keep reminding me
That everything that has been
Is what again will be—
For there is nothing that is new
Beneath God's timeless sun,
And present, past, and future
Are all molded into one—

And east and west and north and south
The same wind keeps on blowing,
While rivers run on endlessly
Yet the sea's not overflowing—
And the restless unknown longing
Of my searching soul won't cease
Until God comes in glory
And my soul at last finds peace.

God, Grant Me the Glory
of "Thy Gift"

God, widen my vision so I may see
 the afflictions You have sent to me—
Not as a cross too heavy to wear
 that weighs me down in gloomy despair—
Not as something to hate and despise
 but as a *gift of love* sent in disguise—
Something to draw me closer to You
 to teach me patience and forbearance, too—
Something to show me more clearly the way
 to *serve* You and *love* You more every day—
Something priceless and precious and rare
 that will keep me forever *safe* in Thy *care*
Aware of the spiritual strength that is mine
 if my selfish, small will is lost in Thine!

Don't Let Me Falter

Oh Lord, don't let me falter—
    Don't let me lose my way;
Don't let me cease to carry
    My burden, day by day
Oh Lord, don't let me stumble—
    Don't let me fall and quit
Oh Lord, please help me find my "job"
    And help me shoulder it.

A Prayer for Patience

God, teach me to be patient—
Teach me to go slow—
Teach me how to "wait on You"
When my way I do not know
Teach me sweet forbearance
When things do not go right
So I remain unruffled
When others grow uptight
Teach me how to quiet
My racing, rising heart
So I may hear the answer
You are trying to impart
Teach me to *let go*, dear God,
And pray undisturbed until
My heart is filled with inner peace
And I learn to know *Your will!*

God, Are You Really Real?

I want to believe
I want to be true
I want to be loyal
And faithful to You,
But where can I go
When vague doubts arise
And when "evil" appears
In an "Angel's disguise"
While clamoring voices
Demand my attention
And the air is polluted
With cries of dissension,
You know, God, it's easy
Just to follow the crowd
Who are "doing their thing"
While shouting out loud
Gross protestations
Against the "old rules"
That limit and hamper
The new freedom schools . . .
God, answer this prayer
And tell me the truth—
Are You really the God
Of both Age and Youth?
And, God, speak to my heart
So I truly feel
That "these prophets" are false
But *You really are real!*

31

Make me a Channel of
Blessing Today

"Make me a channel of blessing today,"
I ask again and again when I pray . . .
Do I turn a deaf ear to the Master's voice
Or refuse to heed His directions and choice?
I only know at the end of the day
That I did so little to *"Pay my way!"*

The Answer

In the tiny petal
   of a tiny flower
      that grew from a tiny pod . . .

Is the miracle
   and the mystery
      of all creation and God!

Open My Eyes

God, open my eyes
    so I may see
And feel Your presence
    close to me . . .
Give me strength
    for my stumbling feet
As I battle the crowd
    on life's busy street,
And widen the vision
    of my unseeing eyes
So in passing faces
    I'll recognize

34

Not just a stranger,
        unloved and unknown,
But a friend with a heart
        that is much like my own . . .
Give me perception
        to make me aware
That scattered profusely
        on life's thoroughfare
Are the best gifts of God
        that we daily pass by
As we look at the world
        with an unseeing eye.

Not to Seek, Lord, but to Share

Dear God, much too often
  we seek You in prayer
Because we are wallowing
  in our own self-despair

We make every word
     we lamentingly speak
An imperative plea
     for whatever we seek
We pray for ourselves
     and so seldom for others,
We're concerned with our problems
     and not with our brother's
We seem to forget, Lord,
     that the "sweet hour of prayer"
Is not for self-seeking
     but to place in Your care
All the lost souls
     unloved and unknown
And to keep praying for them
     until they're Your own
For it's never enough
     to seek God in prayer
With no thought of others
     who are lost in despair
So teach us, dear God,
     that the Power of Prayer
Is made stronger by placing
     the world in Your care!

Prayers Can't Be Answered
Unless They Are Prayed

Life without purpose
    is barren indeed—
There can't be a harvest
    unless you plant seed,
There can't be attainment
    unless there's a goal,

And man's but a robot
       unless there's a soul . . .
If we send no ships out,
       no ships will come in,
And unless there's a contest,
       nobody can win . . .
For games can't be won
       unless they are played,
And prayers can't be answered
       unless they are *prayed* . . .
So whatever is wrong
       with your life today,
You'll find a solution
       if you kneel down and pray
Not just for pleasure,
       enjoyment and health,
Not just for honors
       and prestige and wealth . . .
But pray for a purpose
       to make life worth living,
And pray for the joy
       of unselfish giving,
For great is your gladness
       and rich your reward
When you make your life's purpose
       the choice of the Lord.

God's Stairway

Step by step we climb day by day
Closer to God with each prayer we pray
For "the cry of the heart" offered in prayer
Becomes just another "Spiritual Stair"
In the "Heavenly Staircase" leading us to
A beautiful place where we live anew . . .
So never give up for it's worth the climb
To live forever in "Endless Time"
Where the soul of man is safe and free
To live in love through eternity!

You Helped Us Before,
God, Help Us Again

"O GOD, OUR HELP IN AGES PAST,
OUR HOPE IN YEARS TO BE"—
Look down upon this present
And see our need of Thee . . .
For in this age of unrest,
With danger all around,
We need Thy hand to lead us
To higher, safer ground . . .
We need Thy help and counsel
To make us more aware
That our safety and security
Lie solely in Thy care . . .
Give us strength and courage
To be honorable and true
Practicing Your precepts
In everything we do,
And keep us gently humble
In the greatness of Thy love
So someday we are fit to dwell
With Thee in Peace above.

Thank God for Little Things

Thank You, God, for little things
 that often come our way—
The things we take for granted
 but don't mention when we pray—
The unexpected courtesy,
 the thoughtful, kindly deed—
A hand reached out to help us
 in the time of sudden need—
Oh, make us more aware, dear God,
 of little daily graces
That come to us with "sweet surprise"
 from never-dreamed-of places.

God, Grant Us Hope and Faith and Love

Hope for a world
    grown cynically cold,
Hungry for power
    and greedy for gold . . .

Faith to believe
    when within and without
There's a nameless fear
    in a world of doubt . . .

Love that is bigger
    than race or creed,
To cover the world
    and fulfill each need . . .

God, grant these gifts
    Of faith, hope, and love—
Three things this world
    Has so little of . . .
For only these gifts
    From our Father above
Can turn man's sins
    From hatred to *love!*

"On the Wings of Prayer"

Just close your eyes
    and open your heart
And feel your worries
    and cares depart,
Just yield yourself
    to the Father above
And let Him hold you
    secure in His love—
For life on earth
    grows more involved
With endless problems
    that can't be solved—
But God only asks us
    to do our best,
Then He will "take over"
    and finish the rest—
So when you are tired,
    discouraged, and blue,
There's always one door
    that is open to you—
And that is the door
    to "The House of Prayer"
And you'll find God waiting
    to meet you there,
And "The House of Prayer"
    is no farther away
Than the quiet spot
    where you kneel and pray—

For the heart is a temple
        when God is there
As we place ourselves
        in His loving care,
And He hears every prayer
        and answers each one

When we pray in His name
        "Thy will be done"—
And the burdens that seemed
        too heavy to bear
Are lifted away
        on "the wings of prayer."

A Prayer for Humility

Take me and break me and make me, dear God,
Just what you want me to be—
Give me the strength to accept what You send
And eyes with the vision to see
All the small arrogant ways that I have
And the vain little things that I do,

Make me aware that I'm often concerned
More with myself than with You,
Uncover before me my weakness and greed
And help me to search deep inside
So I may discover how easy it is
To be selfishly lost in my pride—
And then in Thy goodness and mercy
Look down on this weak, erring one
And tell me that I am forgiven
For all I've so willfully done,
And teach me to humbly start following
The path that the dear Saviour trod
So I'll find at the end of life's journey
"A Home in the city of God."

Teach Us to Live

God of love—Forgive! Forgive!
Teach us how to truly live,
Ask us not our race or creed,
Just take us in our hour of need,
And let us know You love us, too,
And that we are a part of You . . .
And someday may man realize
That all the earth, the seas, and skies
Belong to God who made us all,
The rich, the poor, the great, the small,
And in the Father's Holy Sight
No man is yellow, black, or white,
And peace on earth cannot be found
Until we meet on common ground
And every man becomes a brother
Who worships God and loves all others.

Give Us Daily Awareness

On life's busy thoroughfares
We meet with angels unawares—
So, Father, make us kind and wise
So we may always recognize
The blessings that are ours to take,
The friendships that are ours to make
If we but open our heart's door wide
To let the sunshine of love inside.

When Troubles Assail You,
God Will Not Fail You

When life seems empty
And there's no place to go,
When your heart is troubled
And your spirits are low,
When friends seem few
And nobody cares
There is always God
To hear your prayers—
And whatever you're facing
Will seem much less
When you go to God
And confide and confess,
For the burden that seems
Too heavy to bear
God lifts away
On the wings of prayer—
And seen through God's eyes
Earthly troubles diminish
And we're given new strength
To face and to finish
Life's daily tasks
As they come along
If we pray for strength
To keep us strong—
So go to Our Father
When troubles assail you
For His grace is sufficient
And He'll never fail you.

"Now I Lay Me Down to Sleep"

I remember so well this prayer that I said
Each night as my mother tucked me into bed,
And today this same prayer is still the best way
To "sign off with God" at the end of the day
And to ask Him your soul to safely keep
As you wearily close tired eyes in sleep
Feeling content that the Father Above
Will hold you secure in His great arms of love . . .
And having His promise that if ere you wake
His angels will reach down your sweet soul to take
Is perfect assurance that awake or asleep
God is always right there to tenderly keep

All of His children ever safe in His care
For God's here and He's there and He's *everywhere* . . .
So into His hands each night as I sleep
I commit my soul for the dear Lord to keep
Knowing that if my soul should take flight
It will soar to "the Land where there is no night."

Poems of Hope

Grief is a solitary journey. No one but you can know how great the hurt is. No one but you can know the gaping hole left in your life when someone you love has died. And no one but you can mourn the silence that was once filled with laughter and song.

It is the nature of love and of death to touch every person in a totally unique way. Comfort comes from knowing that other people have made the same journey. And solace comes from understanding how others have learned to sing again.

Helen Steiner Rice knew sorrow and grief. She learned early what it meant to lose someone she loved dearly. Many of her poems speak of her pain and grief.

But her poems also reflect hope rediscovered. Hope that struggles, like a crocus through the snow, to overcome the bleak winter of despair. They speak of God's Love, the promise of new beginnings, and of peace that passes understanding.

May you find the same hope and peace in her poems.

Nothing on Earth Is Forever Yours— Only the Love of the Lord Endures!

Everything in life is passing
    and whatever we possess
Cannot endure forever
    but ends in nothingness.

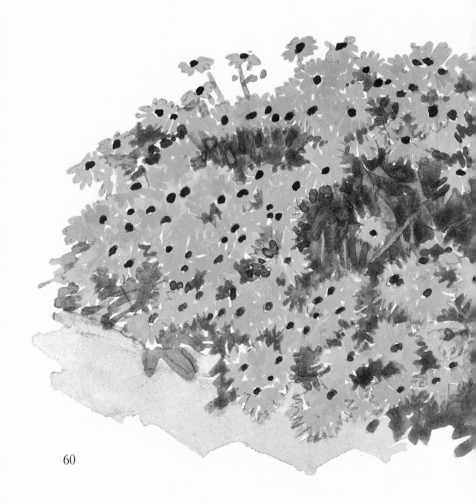

For there are no safety boxes
    nor vaults that can contain
The possessions we collected
    and desire to retain . . .
So all that man acquires,
    be it power, fame, or jewels,
Is but limited and earthly,
    only "treasure made for fools."
For only in God's Kingdom
    can man find enduring treasure,
Priceless gifts of love and beauty—
    more than mortal man can measure.
And the "riches" he accumulates
    he can keep and part with never,
For only in God's Kingdom
    do our treasures last forever . . .
So use the word *forever*
    with sanctity and love,
For nothing is forever
    but *the Love of God above!*

Life Is Forever:
Death Is a Dream!

If we did not go to sleep at night
We'd never awaken to see the light
And the joy of watching a new day break
Or meeting the dawn by some quiet lake
Would never be ours unless we slept
While God and all His angels kept
A vigil through this "little death"
That's over with the morning's breath—
And death, too, is a time of sleeping
For those who die are in God's keeping
And there's a "sunrise" for each soul
For Life not death is God's promised goal—
So trust God's promise and doubt Him never
For only through death can man live forever!

I Do Not Go Alone

If death should beckon me with outstretched hand
And whisper softly of an unknown land
I shall not be afraid to go
For though the path I do not know,
I take death's hand without a fear,
For He who safely brought me here
Will also take me safely back.
And though in many things I lack,
He will not let me go alone
Into the "Valley that's unknown" . . .
So I reach out and take death's hand
And journey to the *"Promised Land."*

Kings and kingdoms all pass away—
Nothing on earth endures . . .
But the love of God who sent His son
Is forever and ever yours!

Spring Awakens What Autumn Puts to Sleep

A garden of asters of varying hues,
Crimson-pinks and violet-blues,
Blossoming in the hazy Fall
Wrapped in Autumn's lazy pall—
But early frost stole in one night
And like a chilling, killing blight
It touched each pretty aster's head
And now the garden's still and dead
And all the lovely flowers that bloomed
Will soon be buried and entombed
In Winter's icy shroud of snow
But oh, how wonderful to know
That after Winter comes the Spring
To breathe new life in everything,
And all the flowers that fell in death
Will be awakened by Spring's breath—
For in God's Plan both men and flowers
Can only reach "bright, shining hours"
By dying first to rise in glory
And prove again the Easter Story.

Death Is a Doorway

On the "Wings of death"
    the "soul takes flight"
Into the land where
    "there is no night"—
For those who believe
    what the Saviour said
Will rise in glory
    though they be dead . . .
So death comes to us
    just to "open the door"
To the Kingdom of God
    and life evermore.
Every mile we walk in sorrow
    Brings us nearer to God's tomorrow!

"Because He Lives . . .
We, Too, Shall Live"

In this restless world of struggle
    it is very hard to find
Answers to the questions
    that daily come to mind—
We cannot see the future
    what's beyond is still unknown
For the secret of God's kingdom
    still belongs to Him alone
But He granted us salvation
    when His Son was crucified
For life became immortal
    because our Saviour died.
Life is not a transient thing—
    It is *change* but never *loss*
For Christ purchased our salvation
    When He died upon the *Cross*

There's Always a Springtime

After the Winter comes the Spring
To show us again that in everything
There's always renewal divinely planned,
Flawlessly perfect, the work of God's Hand . . .
And just like the seasons that come and go
When the flowers of Spring lay buried in snow,
God sends to the heart in its winter of sadness
A springtime awakening of new hope and gladness,
And loved ones who sleep in a season of death
Will, too, be awakened by God's life-giving breath.
All who believe in God's mercy and grace
Will meet their loved ones face to face
Where time is endless and joy unbroken
And only the words of God's love are spoken.

When I Must Leave You

When I must leave you
for a little while,
Please do not grieve
and shed wild tears
And hug your sorrow
to you through the years,
But start out bravely
with a gallant smile;
And for my sake
and in my name
Live on and do
all things the same.
Feed not your loneliness
on empty days,
But fill each waking hour
in useful ways,
Reach out your hand
in comfort and in cheer
And I in turn will comfort you
and hold you near;
And never, never
be afraid to die,
For I am waiting
for you in the sky!
We part with our loved ones
but not forever
If we trust God's promise
and doubt it never.

Each Spring, God Renews
His Promise

Long, long ago in a land far away,
There came the dawn of the first Easter Day,
And each year we see that promise reborn
That God gave the world on that first Easter Morn . . .
For in each waking flower and each singing bird,
The Promise of Easter is witnessed and heard,
And Spring is God's way of speaking to men
And renewing the promise of Easter again,
For death is a season that man must pass through
And, just like the flowers, God wakens him, too . . .
So why should we grieve when our loved ones die,
For we'll meet them again in a "cloudless sky"—
For Easter is more than a beautiful story,
It's the promise of life and Eternal Glory.

Death Is Only a Part of Life

We enter this world
    from "the great unknown"
And God gives each spirit
    a form of its own
And endows this form
    with a heart and a soul
To spur man on
    to his ultimate goal . . .
For all men are born
    to return as they came
And birth and death
    Are in essence the same
And man is but born
    to die and arise
For beyond this world
    in beauty there lies
The purpose of death
    which is but to gain
Life everlasting
    in God's great domain . . .
And no one need make
    this journey alone
For God has promised
    to take care of His own.

Death "bursts our chrysalis of clay"
    so that our soul is free
To soar toward *eternity*
    to dwell in *peace with Thee!*

On the Other Side of Death

Death is a gateway
    we all must pass through
To reach that Fair Land
    where the soul's born anew.
For man's born to die
    and his sojourn on earth
Is a short span of years
    beginning with birth . . .
And like pilgrims we wander
    until death takes our hand
And we start on our journey
    to God's Promised Land.
A place where we'll find
    no suffering nor tears,
Where time is not counted
    by days, months or years . . .
And in this Fair City
    that God has prepared

Are unending joys
  to be happily shared
With all of our loved ones
  who patiently wait
On Death's other side
  to open "the gate"!

Live for "Me"
  And die for "Me"
And I, Thy God,
  Will set you *free!*

Death Opens the Door
to Life Evermore

We live a short while on earth below,
Reluctant to die for we do not know
Just what "dark death" is all about
And so we view it with fear and doubt
Not certain of what is around the bend
We look on death as the final end
To all that made us a mortal being
And yet there lies just beyond our seeing
A beautiful life so full and complete
That we should leave with hurrying feet
To walk with God by sacred streams
Amid beauty and peace beyond our dreams—
For all who believe in the risen Lord
Have been assured of this reward
And death for them is just "graduation"
To a higher realm of wide elevation—
For life on earth is a transient affair,
Just a few brief years in which to prepare
For a life that is free from pain and tears
Where time is not counted by hours or years—
For death is only the method God chose
To colonize heaven with the souls of those
Who by their apprenticeship on earth
Proved worthy to dwell in the land of new birth—
So death is not sad . . . it's a time for elation,
A joyous transition . . . the soul's emigration
Into a place where the soul's safe and free
To live with God through Eternity!

When death steps in, new life begins
And we rise above our temptations and sins!

Life Is Eternal

"Life is eternal," the good Lord said,
So do not think of your loved ones as dead—
For death is only a stepping-stone
To a beautiful life we have never known.
A place where God promised man he would be
Eternally happy and safe and free,
A wonderful land where we live anew
When our journey on earth is over and through—
So trust in God and doubt Him never
For all who love Him live forever,
And while we cannot understand
Just let the Saviour take your hand,
For when death's angel comes to call
"God is so great and we're so small" . . .
And there is nothing you need fear
For faith in God makes all things clear.

"In Him We Live and Move and Have Our Being"

We walk in a world that is strange and unknown
And in the midst of the crowd we still feel alone,
We question our purpose, our part, and our place
In this vast land of mystery suspended in space,
We probe and explore and try hard to explain
The tumult of thoughts that our minds entertain . . .
But all of our probings and complex explanations
Of man's inner feelings and fears and frustrations
Still leave us engulfed in the "mystery of life"
With all of its struggles and suffering and strife,
Unable to fathom what tomorrow will bring—
But there is one truth to which we can cling,
For while life's a mystery man can't understand
The "Great Giver of Life" is holding our hand
And safe in His care there is no need for seeing
For "in Him we live and move and have our being."

In God's Tomorrow There Is Eternal Spring

All nature heeds the call of Spring
As God awakens everything,
And all that seemed so dead and still
Experiences a sudden thrill
As Springtime lays a magic hand
Across God's vast and fertile land—
Oh, how can anyone stand by
And watch a sapphire Springtime sky
Or see a fragile flower break through
What just a day ago or two
Seemed barren ground still hard with frost,
But in God's world no life is lost,
And flowers sleep beneath the ground
But when they hear Spring's waking sound
They push themselves through layers of clay
To reach the sunlight of God's Day—
And man, like flowers, too, must sleep
Until he is called from the "darkened deep"
To live in that place where angels sing
And where there is eternal spring!

God Needed an Angel in Heaven

When Jesus lived upon the earth
      so many years ago,
He called the children close to Him
      because He loved them so . . .
And with that tenderness of old,
      that same sweet, gentle way,
He holds your little loved one close
      within His arms today . . .
And you'll find comfort in your faith
      that in His Home above
The God of little children
      gives your little one His love . . .
So think of your little darling
      lighthearted and happy and free
Playing in God's Promised Land
      where there is joy eternally.

The Tiny "Rosebud" God Picked to Bloom in Heaven

The Master Gardener
From Heaven above
Planted a seed
In the garden of love
And from it there grew
A rosebud small
That never had time
To open at all,
For God in His perfect
And all-wise way
Chose this rose
For His heavenly bouquet
And great was the joy
Of this tiny rose
To be the one our Father chose
To leave earth's garden
For One on high
Where roses bloom always
And never die . . .
So, while you can't see
Your precious rose bloom,
You know the Great Gardener
From the "Upper Room"
Is watching and tending
This wee rose with care,

Tenderly touching
Each petal so fair . . .
So think of your darling
With the angels above
Secure and contented
And surrounded by love,
And remember God blessed
And enriched your lives, too,
For in dying your darling
Brought Heaven closer to you!

Mothers Never Die—They Just Keep House Up in the Sky

When we are children, we are happy and gay
And our mother is young and she laughs as we play,
Then as we grow up, she teaches us truth
And lays life's foundation in the days of our youth—
And then it is time for us to leave home
But her teachings go with us wherever we roam,
For all that she taught us and all that we did
When we were so often just a "bad, little kid"
We will often remember and then realize
That mothers are special and wonderfully wise . . .
And as she grows older, we look back with love
Knowing that mothers are *"Gifts from above,"*
And when she "goes home" to receive her reward
She will dwell in God's Kingdom and "keep house for the Lord"
Where she'll "light up" the stars that shine through the night
And keep all the moonbeams "sparkling and bright"
And then with the dawn she'll put the darkness away
As she "scours" the sun to new brilliance each day . . .
So dry tears of sorrow, for mothers don't die—
They just move in with God and "keep house in the sky,"
And there in God's Kingdom, mothers watch from above
To welcome their children with their undying love!

"Why Should He Die
for Such as I?"

In everything both great and small
We see the hand of God in all.
And in the miracles of Spring
When everywhere in everything
His handiwork is all around
And every lovely sight and sound
Proclaims the God of earth and sky
I ask myself, "Just who am I
That God should send His only Son
That my salvation would be won
Upon a Cross by a sinless Man
To bring fulfillment to God's plan."
For Jesus suffered, bled, and died
That sinners might be sanctified,
And to grant God's children such as I
Eternal life in that *home on high*.

All Nature Proclaims
Eternal Life

Flowers sleeping 'neath the snow,
Awakening when the Spring winds blow;
Leafless trees so bare before,
Gowned in lacy green once more;
Hard, unyielding, frozen sod
Now softly carpeted by God;
Still streams melting in the Spring,
Rippling over rocks that sing;
Barren, windswept, lonely hills
Turning gold with daffodils . . .
These *miracles* are all around
Within our sight and touch and sound,
As true and wonderful today
As when "the stone was rolled away"
Proclaiming to all doubting men
That in God all things live again.

"I Know That My Redeemer Liveth"

They asked me how I know it's true
That the Saviour lived and died . . .
And if I believe the story
That the Lord was crucified?
And I have so many answers
To prove His Holy Being,
Answers that are everywhere
Within the realm of seeing . . .
The leaves that fell at Autumn
And were buried in the sod
Now budding on the tree boughs
To lift their arms to God . . .
The flowers that were covered
And entombed beneath the snow
Pushing through the "darkness"
To bid the Spring "hello" . . .
On every side Great Nature
Retells the Easter Story—
So who am I to question
"The Resurrection Glory."

Heaven is real—it's a *"positive place"*
Where those who believe meet God face to face!

The Legend of the Raindrop

The legend of the raindrop
    has a lesson for us all
As it trembled in the heavens
    questioning whether it should fall—
For the glistening raindrop argued
    to the genie of the sky,
"I am beautiful and lovely
    as I sparkle here on high,
And hanging here I will become
    part of the rainbow's hue
And I'll shimmer like a diamond
    for all the world to view" . . .
But the genie told the raindrop,
    "Do not hesitate to go,
For you will be more beautiful
    if you fall to earth below,
For you will sink into the soil
    and be lost a while from sight,
But when you reappear on earth,
    you'll be looked on with delight;
For you will be the raindrop
    that quenched the thirsty ground
And helped the lovely flowers
    to blossom all around
And in your resurrection
    you'll appear in queenly clothes
With the beauty of the lily
    and the fragrance of the rose;
Then, when you wilt and wither,
    you'll become part of the earth
And make the soil more fertile
    and give new flowers birth" . . .

For there is nothing ever lost
        or eternally neglected,
For everything God ever made
        Is always resurrected;
So trust God's all-wise wisdom
        and doubt the Father never,
For in His Heavenly Kingdom
        There is nothing lost forever.

"I Am the Way, the Truth, and the Life"

I am the way
    so just follow Me
Though the way be rough
    and you cannot see . . .

I am the Truth
    which all men seek
So heed not "false prophets"
    nor the words that they speak . . .

I am the Life
    and I hold the key
That opens the door
    to Eternity . . .

And in this dark world
    I am the light
To the Promised Land
    Where there is no night!

As Long As You Live and Remember— Your Loved One Lives in Your Heart!

May tender memories
　　soften your grief,
May fond recollection
　　bring you relief,
And may you find comfort
　　and peace in the thought
Of the joy that knowing
　　your loved one brought—
For time and space
　　can never divide
Or keep your loved one
　　from your side
When memory paints
　　in colors true
The happy hours
　　that belonged to you.

A Consolation Meditation

On the wings
    of death and sorrow
God sends us
    new hope for tomorrow
And in His mercy
    and His grace
He gives us strength
    to bravely face
The lonely days
    that stretch ahead
And know our loved one
    is not dead
But only sleeping
    and out of our sight
And we'll meet in that land
    Where there is no night

In the Hands of God Even Death Is a Time for Rejoicing

And so when death brings weeping
   and the heart is filled with sorrow,
It beckons us to seek God
   as we ask about "tomorrow"
And in these hours of "heart-hurt"
   we draw closer to believing.
That even death in God's hands
   is not a cause for grieving
But a time for joy in knowing
   death is just a stepping-stone
To a life that's everlasting
   such as we have never known.